ROTHERHAM LIBRARY & INFORMATION SERVICES

This book must be returned by the date specified at the time of issue as the DATE DUE FOR RETURN.

The loan may be extended (personally, by post or telephone) for a further period if the book is not required by another reader, by quoting the above number / author / title.

LIS7a

Acknowledgements

Dedicated to Jim Marriott and Jane Foster for making this possible.

© 2005 Folens Limited, on behalf of the author.

United Kingdom: Folens Publishers, Apex Business Centre, Boscombe Road, Dunstable, LU5 4RL.
Email: folens@folens.com

Ireland: Folens Publishers, Greenhills Road, Tallaght, Dublin 24.
Email: info@folens.ie

Poland: JUKA, ul. Renesansowa 38, Warsaw 01-905.

Folens allows photocopying of pages marked 'copiable page' for educational use, providing that this use is within the confines of the purchasing institution. Copiable pages should not be declared in any return in respect of any photocopying licence.

Editor: Nina Randall
Layout artist: Suzanne Ward
Illustrations: Jim Peacock
Cover design: Martin Cross

First published 2005 by Folens Limited.

Every effort has been made to contact copyright holders of material used in this publication. If any copyright holder has been overlooked, we should be pleased to make any necessary arrangements.

British Library Cataloguing in Publication Data. A catalogue record for this publication is available from the British Library.

ISBN 1 84303 793 9

Contents

Introduction

Year Four
This book is intended to fit very closely to the QCA schemes of work in RE. There are four units within the Year Four schemes. These are:

Unit 4A – How and why do Hindus worship at home and in the mandir?
Unit 4B – Celebrations: Christmas journeys
Unit 4C – Why is Easter important for Christians?
Unit 4D – What religions are represented in our neighbourhood?

In each unit there will be a focus upon the following objectives:

Unit 4A
Beliefs in God
Gods and goddesses
Puja
The mandir/A Hindu shrine

Unit 4B
Bethlehem
Mary and Joseph
The shepherds/The three wise men
Herod

Unit 4C
Palm Sunday
The Last Supper
Gethsemane
The Crucifixion
Easter morning

Unit 4D
Religious groups
What is religion?

This book provides detailed teacher notes and suggested activities based on the QCA schemes of work. Each QCA unit is expected to cover half a term's work and six hours of lessons. The materials within the book cover many of the learning objectives within each QCA unit. They build on knowledge and skills acquired in previous years.

Each unit of work in the book includes a page of teacher notes, which provides the knowledge required to teach the lesson. There then follows a starting point for discussion and two or three differentiated activities that relate or introduce the worksheets, which link specifically to the learning objectives included in the QCA units.

Photocopiable worksheets are provided to enable the pupils to complete the activities. The plenary is intended to review the information learned in the lesson.

Beliefs in God

Learning objectives

Children should:
- understand the meaning of the aum symbol and its significance for Hindus
- learn about some aspects of Hindu beliefs in God.

Background

Hindus believe in one God but worship many gods and goddesses. They believe that the faith's many deities are all aspects of one Supreme Being.

Hindus believe that the sacred symbol or sound – aum – existed at the beginning of time and that the vibrations caused by its sound brought about the creation of the world. This syllable is uttered at the start of all rituals and at the start of meditation. The three letters stand for the three parts of the Trimurti; 'A' represents Brahma, 'U' stands for Vishnu and 'M' is Shiva.

Most Hindus devote the majority of prayer time to one god or goddess. It is often one that has been worshipped by previous generations of their families. When a child is born, Hindus may take their child to a temple to see the local mother goddess shrine, where they receive a special blessing. Hindus also pray to gods and goddesses who control specific aspects of their lives.

Activities

Starting points	Pour some hot water into two glasses. Add salt to one of them. Swap them around so that the children do not know which one has salt in it. Compare this to Hindu beliefs about God; that God is everywhere although we can't see Him.
Worksheet 1 (Easy) *'Creation'*	Discuss what God (Brahman) created when He made the world.
Worksheet 2 (Core) *'Control'*	Discuss people who control aspects of our lives.
Worksheet 3 (Challenge) *'Hindu beliefs'*	Recap what the children have found out so far about the Hindu faith. Look at some non-fiction books on Hinduism with them to extend their knowledge.

Plenary

Discuss any new facts that the challenge group found.

Creation

- Hindus believe that the vibrations of the aum sound brought about the creation of the world. Think about all the things that God created and draw them around the aum symbol. Examples might be the moon and the stars.

Control

● Hindus believe that gods and goddesses control specific aspects of their lives. Think about all the people who control your life. An example may be a teacher who tells you when to go out to play. Draw a picture of two of these people and write about them.

My teacher controls when I go out to play and

what work I do each day.

Hindu beliefs

- Create a small book explaining Hindu beliefs to a small child. Include ideas about gods and goddesses, the aum symbol and prayer. You may want to include some of these pictures to help you.

A Hindu praying

Brahma

Aum symbol

Shiva

A Hindu lady

FOLENS RE IN ACTION 4

Gods and goddesses

Learning objectives

Children should:
- learn about the Hindu idea of God in many forms
- reflect on the different aspects of their own character.

Background

Hinduism has hundreds of different gods. Hindus believe that these many gods all come from one Supreme Spirit, Brahman. Brahman is revealed to Hindus as the Trimurti – three gods known as Brahma, the creator, Vishnu, the preserver and Shiva, the destroyer and re-creator. Brahma's sole purpose is creation. He originally had one head but acquired three more when he created a woman. As she tried to hide from him, he grew heads to the right, left and behind so that he could see her constantly. Vishnu maintains the divine order of the universe, keeping the balance between good and evil. He takes the form of ten avatars. Shiva is the destroyer and re-creator. In one of his forms, he brings the cycle of life to an end in order that a new cycle of life may begin.

Goddesses in Hinduism are seen as separate aspects of one being – the mother goddess, Mahadevi – also known as the Great Goddess.

Mahadevi takes the form of many goddesses, most of whom appear as the many consorts of Brahma, Shiva and Vishnu. Saraswati is the goddess of learning and the arts. She is believed to have invented the Sanskrit language in which the Hindu scriptures are written. Saraswati is also known as Vagishvari – the goddess of speech. Lakshmi is the goddess of wealth, beauty and good luck and the consort of Vishnu. Lakshmi appears by his side when he takes on the form of the ten avatars. When he is Rama, she appears as his dutiful wife, Sita. She is considered a bringer of luck and happiness and when her image is carved above house doors, she brings good fortune to all those who live inside. The goddess, Kali, is the consort of Shiva. She usually appears with a weapon and sometimes with the skulls of her victims. She fights evil and all that is bad in the world. Parvati, another of Shiva's consorts, was born out of the rocks or Himalayas. She is gentle, caring and balances Shiva, the destroyer. Durga is known for her battles with demons that often waged wars against the gods. She is also known for her skills in growing plants.

Activities

Starting points	Discuss the different characteristics of the different Hindu gods.
Worksheet 4 (Easy) *'Roles'*	Discuss the different roles that you have: teacher, colleague, friend, daughter, son and so on.
Worksheet 5 (Core) *'Gods and goddesses'*	Look at a range of pictures of Hindu gods and goddesses.
Worksheet 6 (Challenge) *'Research'*	Look at some non-fiction books on Hinduism with the children to find other examples of Hindu gods and goddesses.

Plenary

Ask the children who completed the easy group activity to discuss which roles they have.

Roles

- Draw yourself in the middle of the page. Then label your picture with all the different roles that you have. An example would be 'pupil'.

Gods and goddesses

● Draw a Hindu god or goddess. Investigate what they hold or wear and make sure you label these details on your picture.

Research

6

- Research another Hindu god or goddess. Draw their picture and write about what they are known for and what their qualities are. Use some books to help you.

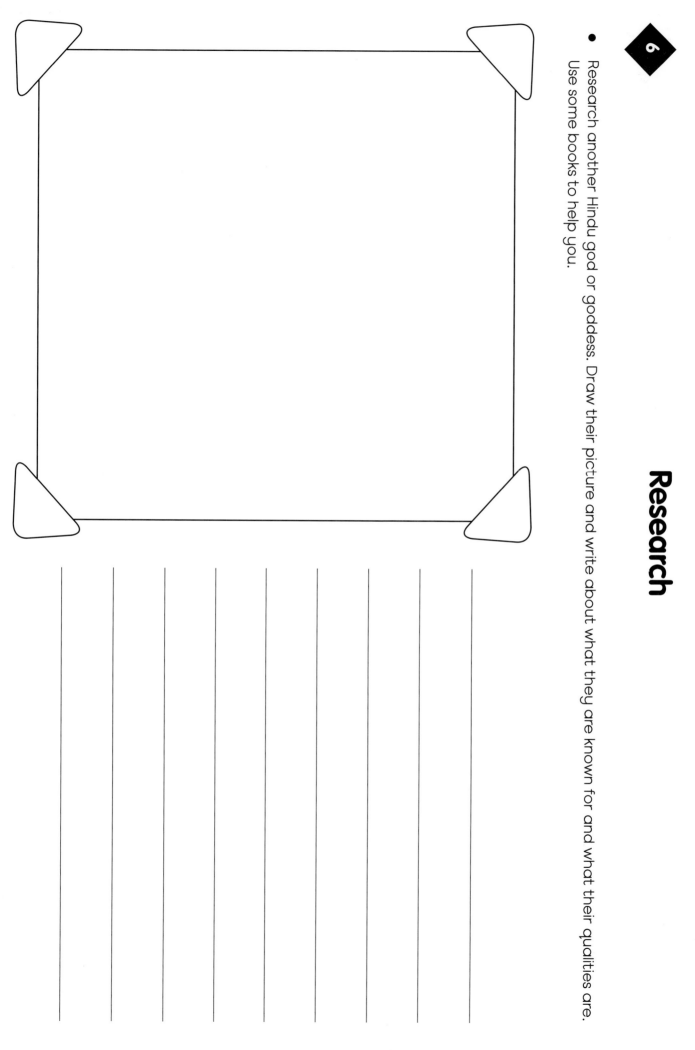

Puja

Learning objectives

Children should:
- understand what 'puja' means
- learn that actions in worship often have symbolic meanings.

Background

Puja is the act of worship. It can take place in the home or at the mandir. The artefacts used in puja are:

1. **An image of a Hindu god** – each home will have a different god at their shrine or temple.
2. **Yantra** – this is a geometric pattern that the family concentrates on as they worship. The meditator's concentration is drawn towards the point at the middle of the interlocking triangles. This point signifies Brahman.
3. **Incense** – this is used to purify the atmosphere.
4. **Food** – often including milk, fruit, nuts, water and flowers. These are considered an offering to God. As soon as the act of worship has finished, these foods are considered to be blessed food. They are then known as prashad. They are offered to worshippers at the shrine.
5. **Arti lamp** – this is a special lamp with five wicks. Each of them is lit and the lamp is waved clockwise in a circle in front of the shrine while the worshippers sing a hymn of praise. The worshippers hold their hands over the sacred fire and then pass them over their forehead with the fire's warmth. In the mandir, this ceremony occurs five times a day.
6. **Bell** – to awaken people's senses for worship.
7. **Whisk** – made with white hair from the tail of an ox.
8. **Aum symbol** – the sacred Hindu sign or word representing God. It is said at the start and end of all prayers.

Activities

Starting points	Think about all the artefacts used during puja. Explore why each artefact is used during the act of worship.
Worksheet 7 (Easy) *'Yantra'*	Look at some examples of yantras. Notice how the triangles look together and the symmetrical pattern they form.
Worksheet 8 (Core) *'Puja'*	Look at some pictures of the artefacts used during puja.
Worksheet 9 (Challenge) *'Hindu worship'*	Recap everything the children have learned about puja.

Plenary

Light some incense so that the children can imagine the atmosphere during puja. Supervise the incense at all times.

Yantra

- Design a yantra. Try to make it symmetrical, ensuring the shapes fit together. An example has been drawn to show you.

Puja

- Draw the artefacts used during puja. Make sure you label them correctly.

Hindu worship

- Think about everything you have learned about Hindu worship. Design a poster using Hindu images and facts. You may want to include a picture of a god or goddess or one of the artefacts used during puja.

FOLENS RE IN ACTION 4 © Folens (copiable page)

The mandir/A Hindu shrine

Learning objectives

Children should:
- learn about worship through the elements, rituals and artefacts that are involved in Hindu worship
- understand that shrines are special places in Hindu homes
- learn about some of the ways that Hindus show devotion to God.

Background

A Hindu temple is called a mandir. When Hindus visit a mandir, they take off their shoes and leave them outside. This shows their respect to the murtis (gods). Hindus start by ringing a bell. This lets the gods know that they are there. Most Hindus have a murti in the mandir that is special to them. They show their love for the murti by offering something. It may be food, milk or incense. They then sip a few drops of holy water.

Only priests are allowed into the shrine. The priests look after the gods with love and devotion. They clean and dress the gods every morning. Priests offer the murtis vegetarian food. When Hindus see a murti in the mandir, they put their hands together in front of their chests and say 'Namaste!' This means 'Honour to you'.

When Hindus pray in the mandir, they bow. Sometimes their foreheads touch the ground. This shows their respect for God.

Every day there is a ceremony called arti. One person moves an arti lamp in front of a murti. The people in the mandir pass their hands over the flame and over their foreheads and hair. As the lamp has been passed in front of the murti, they feel that they have had a blessing from God.

Music is very important to Hindus. Hindu songs of worship are called bhajans. They are sung during the arti ceremony and at festivals. They are often sung in Hindi.

The temple is also a community centre. Rooms are used for meetings and teaching.
When Hindus finish their worship, they share prashad. This is food that has been offered to a god. It is usually sweets, nuts or fruit. It is never meat as Hindus are generally vegetarian.
In a mandir, you will often find offices, a kitchen or dining area and a room for worship.

A Hindu shrine
Hindus believe that the home should also be a temple. Every Hindu home has a shrine. There may be a few pictures on a shelf; or it may take up a whole room. The shrine usually has images or pictures of the gods or goddesses. There is no special day of the week for worship but it usually occurs at least once a day. Early morning before dawn is a good time as it is very peaceful.

Activities

Starting points	Look at some pictures of Hindu shrines. Identify the different artefacts within them.
Worksheet 10 (Easy) *'A special place'*	Hindus often worship in the morning when it is very quiet. Discuss places where the children can go when they want to be quiet or have time to think.
Worksheet 11 (Core) *'A special guest'*	Hindus treat the gods in their home as special guests. Discuss what you can do to make a visitor feel special.
Worksheet 12 (Challenge) *'Hindu glossary'*	Make a list of all the Hindu terms heard so far.

Plenary

Revise all the knowledge acquired on Hinduism during this unit of work.

A special place

- Think about the place where you go to when you want to be quiet or when you want to have some time on your own. It may be your bedroom or just somewhere special you like to visit. Draw a picture of the place and then write about it, saying why it is important to you and what you do when you go there.

FOLENS RE IN ACTION 4   © Folens (copiable page)

A special guest

● Hindus make their chosen god or goddess feel special by offering them food, such as nuts, and milk or incense. The god or goddess is treated as a guest in their home. Think about a time when a special guest visited your home. How did you make them feel special? Write a list of things you did.

1. Made them their favourite meal.

2. _____

3. _____

4. _____

5. _____

6. _____

7. _____

● Now draw a picture of the visitor in your home, enjoying their special time.

Hindu glossary

- Create a glossary for someone who knows nothing at all about Hinduism. What terms would you include to help them? Your first word might be 'aum'.

Word	Meaning
Aum	

FOLENS RE IN ACTION 4

Bethlehem

Learning objectives

Children should:
- understand that people make special journeys to places of religious significance
- learn about the importance of Bethlehem for many Christians.

Background

In biblical times, Bethlehem was just a small village, found about eight kilometres south of Jerusalem. It is the birthplace of two famous people. Israel's King David was born there and so was Jesus, a thousand years later. The place thought to have been where Jesus was born was a cave, used as a stable, on the outskirts of Bethlehem. The Church of the Nativity now covers this cave.

Bethlehem is not the only place that forms part of the Holy Land. Other areas include:
Canaan – also known as the Promised Land. When God brought Moses and the Israelites out of slavery in Egypt, He said that He would lead them to a land that they would call their own. After forty years of wandering in the wilderness, the Israelites arrived in Canaan, a land described as 'flowing with milk and honey' as it was so rich and fertile.
Jerusalem, the city of David – when King David conquered the city in 1000BC, he made it the capital of his kingdom and the centre of worship of the God of Israel. The Ark of the Covenant was also brought to Jerusalem and David's son, Solomon, built the first temple to house it.
Nazareth – Jesus' mother, Mary, and her husband, Joseph, lived in Nazareth. This is where Jesus was brought up. He preached in the local synagogue but was driven out of town, as he was the son of a carpenter.
The River Jordan – the biggest and longest river in Israel. It flows through the Sea of Galilee to the Dead Sea. The Israelites had to cross the River Jordan to get to the Promised Land; John the Baptist washed people in it to cleanse their sins and Jesus was baptised in its waters.
The Dead Sea – a salt lake that lies below sea level, making it the lowest place on earth. It is so salty that no fish can live there. It is believed that the biblical cities of Sodom and Gomorrah are in the Dead Sea area, and that the ruins may be submerged in the lake. Deposits of salt stick out of the water, which remind us of the fate of Lot's wife, who was turned into a pillar of salt.

Activities

Starting points	Look at a map and pictures of the Holy Land. Identify all the places talked about.
Worksheet 13 (Easy) *'Holy places'*	Revise all the places that were talked about at the beginning of the lesson.
Worksheet 14 (Core) *'Journeys'*	Make a list of journeys that the children have made.
Worksheet 15 (Challenge) *'Postcard home…'*	Explore the feelings that a Christian may experience when visiting the Holy Land.

Plenary

Discuss the reasons why pilgrimage is important to many religious believers.

Holy places

- The definitions of the holy places have been mixed up. Cut carefully along the dotted lines and then match the definition to the name. Stick them onto a separate piece of A4 paper.

Bethlehem	The Israelites had to cross it to get to the Promised Land.
Canaan	Where the Ark of the Covenant was taken.
Jerusalem	A salt lake that lies below sea level, making it the lowest place on earth.
Nazareth	The place to which God led Moses and the Israelites.
River Jordan	The birthplace of King David and Jesus.
Dead Sea	Where Jesus was brought up.

Journeys

- Write about a journey that you have made. Think about why you made the journey, whether it was a special one and how you felt when you arrived.

_____

_____

_____

_____

_____

_____

_____

_____

_____

_____

_____

_____

_____

15

Postcard home...

- Imagine that you have been to the Holy Land. Write to a friend describing the places you have seen and the feelings you experienced while you were there.

Mary and Joseph

Learning objectives

Children should:
- understand that the story of the birth of Jesus is of central importance in Christianity and understand some of the reasons why
- know the story of Mary and Joseph's journey to Bethlehem.

Background

Mary was engaged to Joseph, a carpenter in Nazareth. One day, an angel appeared to Mary. Mary was frightened and trembled with fear. The angel told Mary that she would have a son who she would name Jesus and who would be the Son of God. Mary was shocked. She wondered how she could have a child when she was not yet married. She went to stay with her friend, Elizabeth, for three months and then travelled home to Nazareth.

Joseph was surprised to find that Mary was pregnant. He decided that he would no longer marry her, thinking that the child she was carrying was another man's. One day, an angel appeared to him in a dream. The angel told Joseph that the baby was the Son of God and that he should marry Mary as quickly as possible.

Not long before Mary was due to give birth, the Roman Emperor, Augustus, ordered everyone to register in their home towns so that they could be counted in order to work out how much tax should be collected.

Mary and Joseph set off to Bethlehem where Joseph's ancestors had been born. When they arrived, Mary and Joseph were exhausted and looked forward to a good night's sleep at an inn. However, everyone else had had the same idea and, as the town was so crowded, all the rooms were full. Joseph eventually found a stable where Mary could rest.

A short time later, Mary gave birth to her son. She wrapped him in strips of cloth and laid him in a manger so that he could sleep comfortably.

Mary and Joseph were pleased with their new son and named him Jesus, just as the angel had told them.

Activities

Starting points	Discuss how Mary and Joseph would have felt at having to make the journey between Nazareth and Bethlehem.
Worksheet 16 (Easy) *'Timeline'*	Discuss any key vocabulary that the children may need to complete the timeline.
Worksheet 17 (Core) *'Mary and Joseph'*	Recap the main events of the story of Mary and Joseph. Ask the children to retell it using the worksheet.
Worksheet 18 (Challenge) *'I've got a problem...'*	Discuss how Joseph's emotions changed from when he was engaged to Mary, up to when the baby was born.

Plenary

Explore why the birth of Jesus is so important to Christians.

Timeline

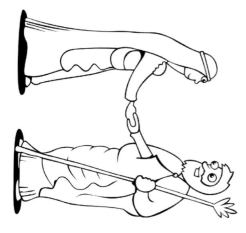

- Plot the events that occurred from the time Mary and Joseph got engaged to when baby Jesus was born. The first one has been done for you.

Mary and Joseph got engaged

Mary and Joseph

- Retell the story of Mary and Joseph using words and pictures.

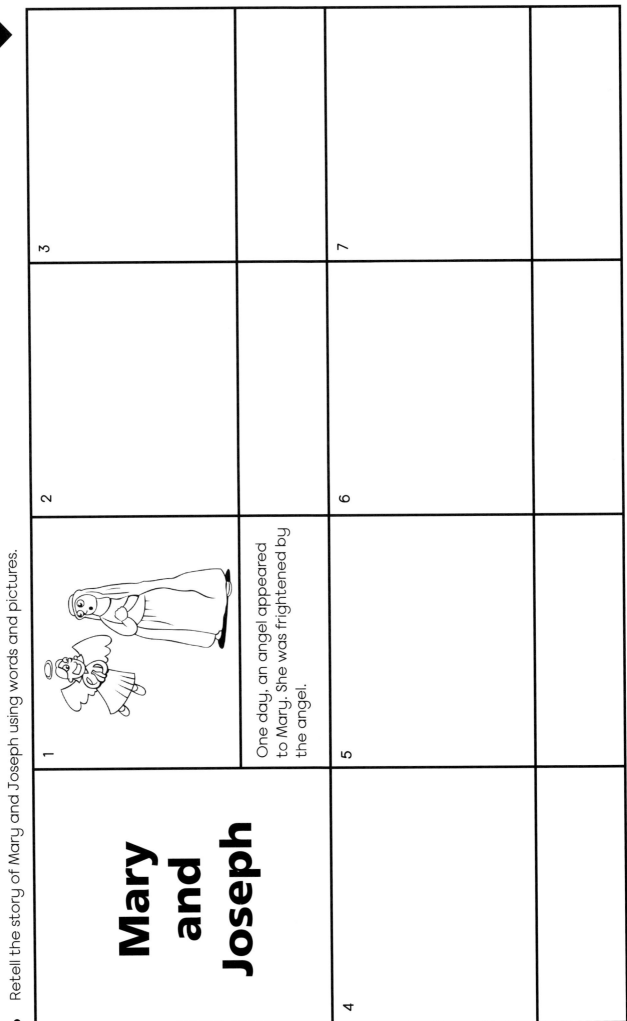

		3
Mary and Joseph	1	2
	One day, an angel appeared to Mary. She was frightened by the angel.	
4	5	6
		7

FOLENS RE IN ACTION 4   27

I've got a problem…

- Think about how Joseph felt. His wife was pregnant with God's child. He had to travel to Bethlehem with Mary and then, when he got there, all the rooms were full. Write a letter to a problem page asking for a solution.

The shepherds/The three wise men

Learning objectives

Children should:

- explain the significance to Christians of key features of the nativity story
- understand that they will have different views of a particular story and that people within a story will have different feelings, hopes and motives
- know that music can be used to give a religious message and to appreciate that the basis of this music is the story they have listened to
- learn about ways in which beliefs and religious ideas can be expressed through words and music, art and literature.

Background

In some fields, shepherds were keeping a watchful eye on their sheep. Suddenly, an angel appeared to them.

The shepherds were frightened but the angel reassured them. The angel told them that that night, the Saviour had been born in the streets of Bethlehem. The shepherds were told to visit the child lying in the manger. As soon as the angel had stopped speaking, the sky was filled with a crowd of angels. When the angels disappeared, the shepherds went to Bethlehem and found Jesus lying in a manger. They paid their respects and left, telling everyone about the wonderful sight that they had seen.

Soon other visitors came looking for Jesus. Wise men from a distant country came to Jerusalem and were soon asking where they could see the new baby that had been born. The wise men had followed a bright star for many days. They wanted to worship the new king and give him some gifts.

When King Herod heard this, he became concerned and started to ask about this new baby. His advisors told him that someone had said that a new king had been born in Bethlehem.

Herod was very clever. He found the three wise men, told them that they would find the new king in Bethlehem and that when they discovered exactly where he was, they should return to Herod in Jerusalem and let him know.

The wise men carried on their journey, following the bright star, which eventually brought them to a stable. When they saw Jesus, they bowed down and offered the gifts they had brought of gold, myrrh and frankincense. Before they left, they had a dream that they should not tell Herod where the new king was and so they returned home without going back to Jerusalem.

Activities

Starting points	Listen to a short extract from Handel's 'Messiah', when the angels appear to the shepherds.
Worksheet 19 (Easy) *'Moods'*	Allow the children to continue to listen to Handel's 'Messiah'. Discuss with them how the music makes them feel.
Worksheet 20 (Core) *'Messiah'*	Brainstorm words that may be useful for an acrostic poem of the word 'Messiah'.
Worksheet 21 (Challenge) *'Visit to see the baby'*	Discuss what people may want to find out about the shepherds' visit to see baby Jesus.

Plenary

Give some children the role of the shepherds in the story. Let the children from the challenge group interview them so that they can complete the answers to their questions.

Moods

- Create a picture that reflects the moods that you feel as you listen to Handel's 'Messiah'. What colours will you use?

Messiah

● Create an acrostic poem for the word 'Messiah'. The first line has been completed for you.

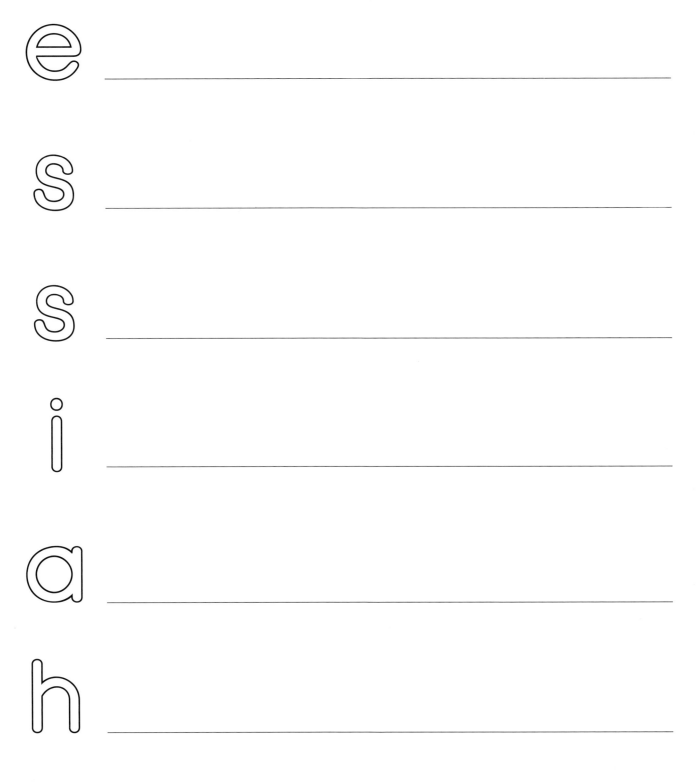

M essages of hope to Christians

e _____

s _____

s _____

i _____

a _____

h _____

FOLENS RE IN ACTION 4

Visit to see the baby

● Imagine that you are working for a local TV company. You are to interview one of the shepherds. What will your questions be? How do you think the shepherds will answer? One question has been done for you.

1. What did the new baby look like?

2. _____

3. _____

4. _____

5. _____

Herod

Learning objective

Children should:
■ understand that although the people in the story lived in a very different world, their emotions would have been similar to those of people today and that fear and jealousy continue to cause problems.

Background

After the wise men had left Bethlehem, an angel appeared to Joseph one night in a dream.

The angel told Joseph to take Mary and Jesus and flee to Egypt as quickly as possible. They were to stay there until the angel told them that it would be safe to return. She added that King Herod had decided that he wanted baby Jesus to be killed and that he would hunt him down until he was dead.
That very night, Joseph woke Mary and Jesus. They wrapped up Jesus warmly and, making sure that they had their possessions, set off for Egypt.

King Herod was waiting anxiously for news from the wise men. They had made a promise to him that they would come back to tell him where they had seen Jesus. When Herod realised that the wise men were not returning and that they had tricked him, he became very angry.

He gathered his soldiers together and told them that they must go into Bethlehem and kill every baby boy under the age of two.

They carried out this task, leaving no baby boy unharmed. King Herod died soon after. Again, an angel appeared to Joseph in a dream. Joseph was told that he could return to Israel where Jesus would be safe, as the person trying to kill him was dead.

When they arrived, they heard that Herod's son was in charge of Judea, so they were afraid to go there. Instead, they travelled further north and settled in the town of Nazareth.

Activities

Starting points	Explore the feelings that Herod may have felt in the story of Jesus' birth. Has there been a time when any of the children have experienced these feelings?
Worksheet 22 (Easy) *'Travels'*	Compare what Mary and Joseph would have packed for their journey with what you took on a journey you have made.
Worksheet 23 (Core) *'Jealousy'*	Discuss reasons why people feel jealous of others. Ask the children if they can remember where it states that we should not be jealous of others' belongings.
Worksheet 24 (Challenge) *'Herod's day'*	Explore Herod's feelings as he realised that the wise men were not coming back.

Plenary

Using a map, look at the route that Mary and Joseph might have taken from Bethlehem to Egypt.

Travels

● Think about everything that Mary and Joseph would have needed to take for the journey from Bethlehem to Egypt. One idea has been included for you.

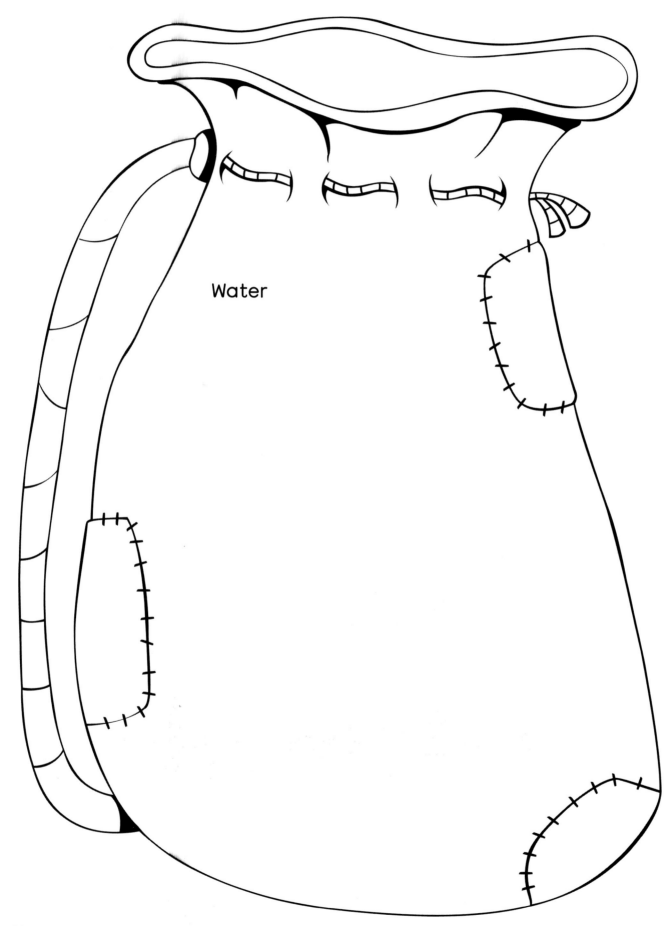

Water

23

Jealousy

● Make a list of situations in which a person may feel jealous of somebody else. One has been done for you.

Jealousy

My friend has got the latest pair of trainers.

Herod's day

● Imagine how Herod felt when he realised that the three wise men were not coming back to tell him where he could find baby Jesus. Write about this and his decision to kill all baby boys under the age of two.

Palm Sunday

Learning objectives

Children should:
- learn about the events of Palm Sunday
- learn about the atmosphere and feelings of the crowd on Palm Sunday
- know that emotions and feelings are involved with decisions and faith.

Background

One day, Jesus was on his way to Jerusalem. As he reached the hill called the Mount of Olives, he told two of his disciples to go ahead. He said that they would see a donkey tied up by a house and that they should untie it and bring it back to him.

As the disciples began to untie the donkey, some villagers appeared and asked what they were doing. The disciples replied that their master, Jesus, needed it. At this, they were left alone to take the donkey. They led the donkey back to Jesus. He mounted it and started to ride into Jerusalem. As Jesus rode into Jerusalem, his followers began to sing, shout and praise God. They thanked Him for all the miracles He had performed.

As they saw Jesus coming, more and more people joined in. They waved palm branches and shouted 'Hosanna!' Soon it seemed as if all of Jerusalem had turned out to see Jesus.

Some Pharisees in the crowd were not impressed. They asked Jesus to tell his disciples to be quiet, but Jesus refused, saying that it was their choice to shout as they did.

Activities

Starting points	Look at some examples of palm crosses.
Worksheet 25 (Easy) *'Palm cross'*	Discuss why Christians have palm crosses at Easter.
Worksheet 26 (Core) *'Hosanna!'*	Discuss how the crowd may have felt as Jesus passed by on Palm Sunday.
Worksheet 27 (Challenge) *'Palm Sunday'*	Recap the events of Palm Sunday.

Plenary

Explore the reasons why the crowd welcomed Jesus.

Palm cross

● Draw your own palm cross. Then explain why Christians have palm crosses at Easter.

Hosanna!

• Decorate the word 'Hosanna!'. Then write adjectives around the word to describe how the crowd may have felt as Jesus passed by on Palm Sunday.

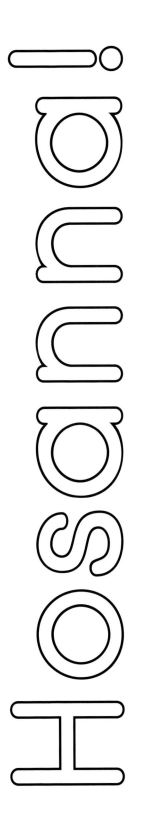

Palm Sunday

- Imagine that you were one of the people in the crowd as Jesus passed by. Write an account, focusing on what you saw and the feelings you experienced.

FOLENS RE IN ACTION 4 © Folens (copiable page)

The Last Supper

Learning objectives

Children should:
- learn about the significance of the Last Supper
- understand that Jesus came as a servant king, not as a ruler.

Background

It was time for the celebration of Passover in Jerusalem. Jesus had told his disciples, Peter and John, to go to a house where they could prepare the Passover meal.

When the disciples and Jesus arrived at the house that evening, Jesus poured some water into a bowl and knelt down at the feet of his disciples. They had had a long journey and their feet were dusty. When Jesus started to wash their feet, they were horrified that their master was behaving like a servant. However, by doing this, Jesus was showing that no one person is better than any other. He told the disciples that they must continue to serve one another in this way.

Shortly after, the disciples sat down to eat. Jesus felt sad. He knew that soon he would return to his Father in heaven. He announced that one of his disciples would betray him. They were shocked and in turn asked if it could be them.

Jesus stated that it would be the one who dipped bread into the bowl with him. Then, dipping the bread, Jesus handed it to Judas, saying, 'What you are about to do, do quickly,' but no one at the meal understood why Jesus had said this to him. Judas left immediately.

Later, Jesus took some bread, thanked God for it and broke it into pieces. He shared it amongst his disciples, saying that it represented his body. He then asked them to drink the wine, saying that they would remember this as his blood when he was gone.

Activities

Starting points	Talk about the Last Supper and explore what Jesus was telling his disciples.
Worksheet 28 (Easy) *'Special meal'*	Discuss reasons why you may ask someone to come for a special meal.
Worksheet 29 (Core) *'How would you help?'*	Discuss the actions of Jesus as he washed his disciples' feet. Why did he do this?
Worksheet 30 (Challenge) *'Eucharist'*	Today, Christians remember Jesus through the Eucharist. Discuss other names for the Eucharist.

Plenary

Explore the reasons why Jesus came as a servant king, not as a ruler.

Special meal

● Write about a time when you shared a special meal with friends. Draw what you had to eat and then write about why it was a special meal.

_____

_____

_____

_____

_____

_____

_____

_____

_____

How would you help?

● Jesus washed his disciples' feet, as he wanted them to help others just as he had done. Imagine that you are one of the disciples. What could you do to help others? One idea has been given.

1. Do the washing up at home.

2. _____

_____

3. _____

_____

4. _____

_____

5. _____

_____

Eucharist

- Christians remember the Last Supper through the Eucharist. Research what the Eucharist involves for Christians today. Write the facts around the chalice, the cup used during the Eucharist. One fact has been included to help you.

The word 'Eucharist' means thanksgiving.

Gethsemane

Learning objective

Children should:
- learn about the events which led to Jesus being arrested.

Background

Jesus knew that he would soon die and tried to prepare his disciples for his death. He told them that he would be going to his Father's house, where he would prepare a place for them. When it was their turn to die, he would come back to collect them. Meanwhile, he would send the Holy Spirit to teach them and remind them of everything that he had said.

Later that evening, he walked with the disciples to the garden of Gethsemane. Jesus was very sad. He knew that his time was near and he asked his disciples to stay awake and pray with him. However, they were tired and, one by one, they fell asleep.

Suddenly, one of Jesus' disciples, Judas, appeared through the bushes. Judas had already arranged to betray Jesus for thirty pieces of silver. He had told the soldiers that they would know who Jesus was as Judas would kiss him on his cheek; a sign of respect for his leader. Soon, Jesus realised what was happening and the soldiers arrested him. Simon Peter, one of the disciples, realised the situation, grabbed his sword and sliced off the ear of one of the high priest's servants.

Jesus was angry with Simon Peter. He told him that if he had wanted to, he could have asked his Father to send some angels to protect him. Jesus touched the servant's ear and it was immediately healed.

Jesus spoke to his captors. He asked them why they had brought their weapons when he would not harm anyone. He reminded them that they had seen him teaching in the temple every day and yet he had not harmed anyone.

Then the soldiers seized Jesus and took him away to the high priest's house. Simon Peter followed at a distance.

Activities

Starting points	Discuss why Jesus needed the disciples to stay awake. How do you think the disciples felt when they realised that they had been asleep when Jesus needed them most?
Worksheet 31 (Easy) *'Disciple needed!'*	Discuss what qualities the disciples had. Why did Jesus choose them?
Worksheet 32 (Core) *'Friends'*	Explore the reasons why Jesus wanted to be with his friends, the disciples, for the last time.
Worksheet 33 (Challenge) *'Disappointment'*	Jesus was sad and disappointed that his disciples had fallen asleep when he needed them to stay awake. Talk about a time when you as a teacher faced disappointment. How did you deal with it?

Plenary

Discuss the events that Jesus experienced before being taken to the high priest's house: his time with the disciples in the garden, Judas' betrayal, his arrest and the actions of Simon Peter. What feelings would he have experienced as each event occurred?

Disciple needed!

● Write an advert for a disciple. Think about the qualities that Jesus would have wanted his disciples to have. Would they have been kind, honest and hard-working?

FOLENS RE IN ACTION 4   © Folens (copiable page)

Friends

- Imagine that you are going to spend one last time with your friends as you are moving away. Where would you take them and why? Would it be bowling or to the cinema?

_____

_____

_____

_____

_____

_____

_____

_____

_____

_____

Disappointment

- Think about a time when you were disappointed. Describe how you felt and state what had happened. An example could be that you arranged to meet a friend in town and they didn't turn up.

CINEMA

film starts
2.00

The Crucifixion

Learning objectives

Children should:
- learn about the events of the Crucifixion
- know about the feelings of the disciples, friends and family of Jesus
- explore the reasons why Jesus was crucified.

Background

After Jesus had been arrested, he was taken to the high priest. Many witnesses were called in the hope that one of them would provide evidence to prove that Jesus should not be killed but none of them could. Jesus stood in silence throughout this time and only spoke when asked if he was the Son of God. Upon agreeing that he was, Jesus was accused of speaking against God and was led away to be sentenced by Pontius Pilate, the Roman Governor.

Unnoticed, Peter had followed the group of soldiers who had arrested Jesus. He sat in the courtyard trying to keep warm. While he was there, three people asked him if he knew Jesus. Every time, he said that he didn't. On the third time of denying him, a cock crowed. Peter remembered Jesus saying earlier in the evening that he would deny Jesus. Peter left the courtyard crying tears of shame and grief.

Meanwhile, Jesus was brought before Pontius Pilate, the only man who could order someone's death. Pontius Pilate wanted to free Jesus. He knew that he presented no harm to the Roman government and thought that he had only been arrested because the chief priest was jealous of him. At the time of Passover, it was a tradition for one prisoner to be set free. Pilate asked the crowd to decide who would be freed, Jesus or a man called Barabbas. The crowd chose Barabbas and Jesus was led away to his death.

When Pilate ordered his soldiers to take Jesus away, they dressed him like a king, with a purple cloak and a crown of thorns. As Jesus walked to his crucifixion in Golgotha, the Roman soldiers forced a passer-by to carry his cross. When they reached Golgotha, they hammered long nails through Jesus' hands and feet and nailed him to the cross. His clothes were shared amongst the soldiers watching below. Despite being in pain, Jesus asked God, his Father, that they should be forgiven.

His mother, Mary, stood watching. At midday, an unusual darkness covered the sky and, three hours later, Jesus died. A man who had been watching, Joseph of Arimathea, went to Pilate and asked for Jesus' body. When Pilate agreed, Joseph took down the body, wrapped it in linen and placed it in a tomb.

Activities

Starting points	Discuss some of the reasons why Jesus was put to death.
Worksheet 34 (Easy) *'Betrayal'*	Discuss the meaning of the word 'betrayal'. Try to think of situations in which people have been betrayed.
Worksheet 35 (Core) *'Sorry!'*	Discuss why Pontius Pilate acted as he did. What feelings would he have experienced after Jesus was put to death?
Worksheet 36 (Challenge) *'Barabbas/Jesus'*	Make a list of the contrasting feelings that the disciples, friends and family of Jesus would have felt.

Plenary

Explore the reasons why Joseph of Arimathea wanted to take Jesus' body away.

Betrayal

- Peter felt guilty because he had let Jesus down. Think about a time when you let someone down. Describe your actions, trying to justify what you did.

Sorry!

● Write a letter from Pontius Pilate to Jesus apologising for his actions.

Dear Jesus,

Barabbas/Jesus

- Contrast the feelings of Barabbas with those of Jesus; Jesus after hearing he was to be crucified, Barabbas after hearing he was to be set free. Two ideas have been given to help you.

Jesus	Barabbas
Upset	Overjoyed

Easter morning

Learning objectives

Children should:
- understand why Christians believe in life after death – resurrection
- learn that the cross and crucifix are symbolic for some Christians
- know about the different ways in which people respond to the Resurrection.

Background

Three days after the crucifixion, Mary Magdalene, Mary (mother of James and John) and Salome (Jesus' friend) made their way to the tomb where Jesus' body lay. As they approached the tomb, they were shocked to see that the stone lid had been pushed to one side. Nervously, they looked inside to find that the body was missing.

When they saw a man sitting at the side of the tomb, dressed in a white robe, they were even more nervous. He told them that they should not be frightened and that Jesus had risen from the dead. He told them that if they travelled quickly to Galilee, they would see Jesus but that, before setting off, they should go to tell Peter and the other disciples what they had seen.

They went back to the disciples and told them everything that had happened that morning.

Meanwhile, Mary Magdalene had gone back to the tomb to take one last look at it. She stood there crying. As she did so, she heard footsteps behind her. She turned around to see a man standing there. Presuming he was the gardener, she asked him where the body of Jesus had been taken. When he spoke, she realised that it was Jesus, risen from the dead. She ran off to tell the others.

Later that day, two women were walking along a path to a small village just outside Jerusalem. Their thoughts were of the crucifixion that had happened a few days earlier. They met a stranger and he asked what they were talking about. They explained and invited him to enjoy a meal with them that evening. While they were eating, the stranger broke bread and gave thanks. They realised that they were eating with Jesus; he disappeared quickly and they returned to tell the disciples what had happened.

The disciples were together that evening when Jesus appeared before them. They were amazed and delighted when they realised who it was.

Jesus showed them the scar marks on his hands. One of the disciples, Thomas, was missing when this happened. He said that he would only believe the others if he could see Jesus and feel the scars on his hands and side. Jesus appeared in the room again. He allowed Thomas to touch the scars and Thomas never doubted again.

Activities

Starting points	Discuss the Resurrection. Talk about why Christians believe in life after death.
Worksheet 37 (Easy) *'Easter celebrations'*	Discuss why some people send cards at Easter. Look at some examples of Easter cards.
Worksheet 38 (Core) *'Easter garden'*	Look at some examples of Easter gardens. Discuss what could be planted in an Easter garden.
Worksheet 39 (Challenge) *'Resurrection'*	Create a list of words that would be suitable for use in a poem about the Resurrection.

Plenary

Recap the different stages of the Easter story.

Easter celebrations

- Design your own Easter card. You may want to use some of the images below. Colour them in, cut them out and then glue them onto some stiff card. Write an appropriate message in the middle of your card.

HAPPY EASTER

FOLENS RE IN ACTION 4

Easter garden

● Design your own Easter garden, thinking about what symbols you could use to remind Christians about the Easter story.

Resurrection

- Create an acrostic poem for the word Resurrection. The first line has been completed for you.

R ose from the dead

e _____

s _____

u _____

r _____

r _____

e _____

c _____

t _____

i _____

o _____

n _____

Religious groups

Learning objectives

Children should:
- use a range of resources to discover which religious traditions are represented in the neighbourhood of the school
- work co-operatively with others.

Background

There are many different religions across the world. Whereas in the past, large populations of one religion could be found in one area of the world, this is no longer so. The majority of Christians today live in developing countries, far from the Middle Eastern and Mediterranean beginnings of Christianity. In many countries, Islam is now the second largest religious group and in other countries, the dominant group.

Within a local community, there may be many religious faiths represented, or only one. Signs and symbols may enable you to judge the predominant faith in an area. For example, in an area where there is a church, you could presume that many inhabitants may be Christians. Where there is a mosque, you may presume that many of the area's inhabitants are Muslims. Other buildings include gurdwaras for Sikhs, synagogues for Jewish people and mandirs for Hindus.

However, this is not always the case. Jews have now been dispersed throughout the world. Therefore, although a synagogue may have been built in a particular place, this does not mean that there are lots of Jews living in that area. One of the ways in which you could judge this is if people wore a sign or symbol of their religion.

Activities

Starting points	Discuss which religions could be represented in your local area. Talk to the children about what research methods they could use to find this out.
Worksheet 40 (Easy) *'Symbols'*	Remind the children how to use research skills to access information about different religions.
Worksheet 41 (Core) *'Places of worship'*	List the religions that you may find in your area.
Worksheet 42 (Challenge) *'A local study'*	Look at a map to identify what the different symbols mean.

Plenary

Discuss all the information found so far. Ask the challenge group to reveal which places of worship can be found in your area.

40

Symbols

- Use books and the Internet to find out what signs or symbols different religions have. Draw these signs or symbols and then label them.

FOLENS RE IN ACTION 4 © Folens (copiable page)

Places of worship

- Use books and the Internet to find out what the places of worship belonging to each religion look like. Draw examples and then label them with the name of the building and the religion of the people who go there.

A local study

- Use a local map to discover which religious buildings can be found in your area. List these and where they are situated.

What is religion?

Learning objectives

Children should:
- learn about the main beliefs, practices, buildings and people of the religious traditions in the neighbourhood of the school
- select and sequence information
- work co-operatively with others.

Background

A religion is a system of beliefs and practices. Judaism, Sikhism, Christianity, Islam and Hinduism all have their own ideas. However, they all offer explanations about the meaning and purpose of life.

Within a community, religion can bring people together. Children are often taught very early about their faith and often have to attend a school attached to their place of worship to learn more about their faith. Within the religious community, members worship together, celebrate festivals and attend other social events. This helps them support one another. This is particularly important for small communities.

All of these religions have sacred books that tell people how they should live their lives. Christians have the Bible, Jews the Torah, Sikhs the Guru Granth Sahib, Muslims the Qur'an and Hindus the Vedas. These books offer guidance and tell worshippers how they should live.

Activities

Starting points	Recap what was found out in the previous lesson. Explain that the children will focus specifically on the religion that predominates in your area.
Worksheet 43 (Easy) *'A religious leader'*	Discuss a range of research skills that the children can use to find out further information about a leader of the religion in your area.
Worksheet 44 (Core) *'How do they worship?'*	Discuss how people may feel when they go to a place of worship.
Worksheet 45 (Challenge) *'Beliefs/practices'*	Discuss why believers in one religion have certain beliefs and practices that they follow.

Plenary

Allow the children to present all the information they have found out about the religion in the neighbourhood of the school.

A religious leader

● Find out everything that you can about the leader of the religion you are researching. What qualities do they need to be the leader? What do they have to do as part of their job? Draw a picture of them and then write about them.

FOLENS RE IN ACTION 4   © Folens (copiable page)

How do they worship?

● Imagine that you are writing a list of rules for a visitor to the place of worship in your area. Think about what they would have to wear and how they would be expected to behave.

Rules

1. _____

_____

_____

2. _____

_____

_____

3. _____

_____

_____

4. _____

_____

_____

5. _____

_____

Beliefs/practices

- Think about all the facts that you have found out about the religion in the neighbourhood of your school. Write them on this sheet around the title.

Beliefs/practices

FOLENS RE IN ACTION 4